# Great North

*A poem
of the
Great North Run*

## Andy Croft

IRON
PRESS

First published May 2001 by
IRON Press
5 Marden Terrace
Cullercoats
North Shields
Northumberland
NE30 4PD
Tel/Fax: 0191 253 1901
E-mail:ironpress@yahoo.com
ISBN 0 90622889 1

Printed by Peterson Printers, South Shields

Typset in New York 9pt

Cover and Book design by IRON Eye @ IRON Press
Photos of Andy Croft by Martin Avery
Gt North Run Photo courtesy of Shields Gazette/NE Press Ltd

IRON Press Books are distributed by
Signature Book Representation Ltd
Sun House, 2 Little Peter St, Manchester M15 4PS
Tel: (0161) 834 8767   Fax: (0161) 834 8656
E-mail: admin@signature-books.co.uk

## Andy Croft

was poet-in-residence on
the Great North Run in 2000.

His many books include *Red
Letter Days*, *Out of Old Earth*, *A
Weapon in Struggle* and
*Selected Poems of Randall
Swingler*.
He has also written nineteen
books for teenagers about
football. His previous
collections of poetry include
*Nowhere Special*, *Gaps Between
Hills*, *Headland* and *Just as Blue*.
He currently works as writer-
in-residence at HMP Holme
House in Stockton. He lives in
Middlesbrough.

# *Acknowledgements*

Thanks are due to the editors of the following publications, where parts of the poem were first published - *Newcastle Journal, The North, Other Poetry, Penniless Press, Prop* and *Runner's World* - and to the audiences who let me try out earlier versions of the poem at readings in Berlin, Bishop Auckland, Byker, Middlesbrough, Morpeth, Newcastle and Stockton

\*

*Andy Croft's Great North Run Residency was funded by*:
Arts Council of England/Year of the Artist
Northern Arts' Millennium Arts Festival
Newcastle and Gateshead Initiative
New Writing North
Northern Rock

\*

Thanks also to Nova International

\*

**~For Nikki, a great North runner~**

# *Introduction*

*Sport and poetry have always gone together. Over two thousand years ago, poets used to write odes for the winners of the games at Delphi, Corinth and Olympus. The first marathon runner, Phidippides, is celebrated in Herodotus. Homer spent a whole book of The Odyssey describing the Phaiacian games.*

*Today however, sport and poetry inhabit different worlds, incompatible if not actually antagonistic. There is a lot of very good writing about watching sport - specifically football - but not much about doing it. Not many poets like running, and not many runners write poetry. We may live in an age of mass sport and mass literacy, but it seems bizarre now to think that between 1912 and 1948 the Olympic Games also included medals for the arts. Although the idea of a Great North Run Poet-in-Residence as part of Northern Arts' Millennium Arts Festival attracted a good deal of press interest, it was mainly tongue-in-cheek journalism, stimulated by the evident comic incompatibility of running and poetry.*

*The idea of a Poet-in-Residence on the Great North Run in 2000 was to help to begin to break down some of these barriers. With almost 50,000 entries, the Great North Run is now the largest half-marathon on the planet, which means that for just one day the North-east of England is the sporting capital of the world, not to mention the known universe. It was also an opportunity to take poetry into an area of popular culture far removed from the usual yoof-culture territory of football, drugs and rock 'n roll. I wanted to work with some of the children through whose streets the Great North Run passes once a year (leaving behind several hundred thousand plastic bottles). The Great North Run belongs to them as much as to the runners. Without the encouragement of the kids who shout 'Wazzaa !' and hold out their hands to be slapped by passing runners, the 13.1 miles from Newcastle to South Shields would seem even longer. I worked in nine schools along the route, three in Gateshead and six in South Tyneside, where we created a 700-line epic poem about the run from the perspective of the kids who wrote it. This was published early in 2001.*

*Having run the Great North Run almost every year since 1988 (best time : 1 hour 50), I have always been dismayed by the TV and journalistic coverage of the event, which concentrates almost entirely on the Olympians at the front, only occasionally pausing to make patronising comments about the guys dressed as chickens at the back. I wanted to write a participant's version of the run, to try to record, celebrate and get under the sweaty skin of this extraordinary event - the runners, organisers, spectators, and wheel-chair participants, the St John's Ambulance volunteers, the traffic police, the bands that play along the way, the months of training and preparation, and all the heroism (and some of the dottiness) that characterises this extraordinary day.*

*Half-marathon running is a very democratic activity ; the whole point is that everyone can have a go. If I can do it, then anyone can. It is a uniquely popular sport, a mass activity that is both collective and non-competitive. In this respect it seems to me to serve as a good model for the arts, for politics and civil society - and for poetry.*

*Andy Croft*
*Spring 2001*

*" To run upon the sharp wind of the North."*
(The Tempest)

# S T A R T

Well this is it - the moment has arrived ;
  No second thoughts, it's time to show your mettle,
It's this for which so many months you've strived,
  It's now or never, time to grasp the nettle,
To show the world the stuff of which you're made,
  To put your preparations to the test,
So here you are, uncertain and afraid,
  In fetching bin-bag, shorts and running vest,
With folk of every shape and every size
  From far-too-thin through medium to weighty,
Who like to take a bit of exercise
  Between the age of seventeen and eighty.
You can't explain just what you're doing here,
  With 40,000 other running nuts,
You're not sure if it's such a good idea,
  Or what exactly's happening in your guts,
Or why, when you could be tucked up in bed,
  You're going to put your body through the trauma
Of running 13.1 miles instead
  (Such thoughts of bed don't make you any warmer)

So this is why you suffered all that training,
  To freeze here on a six-lane motorway
(And now, as if on cue, it's started raining)
  On Tyneside on a cold October day.

Five minutes still to go before the start.
  You rub your calves, and do your best to stretch,
You try to calm your palpitating heart,
  And worry if your nerves will make you retch.
Three minutes. Though you know you've tied your laces
  You tie them tighter, synchronise your watch,
Shake hands, exchange some last good-luck embraces,
  Rub ointment on your legs and in your crotch.
One minute still to go. You diagnose
  A twinge in your left knee you don't recall,
Re-check the time again and touch your toes,
  Decide you need the toilet after all,
When suddenly the starting pistol's fired,
  And this year's Great North Run's at last begun!
And there's no time for feeling stiff or tired
  As 40,000 runners start to run.
Then stop. Then shuffle forward. Stop once more.
  The anti-climax really is quite stunning ;
You stand for several minutes more before
  You move at all, ten more before you're running.
Though no-one really cares about the winners
  The Kenyans up ahead have crossed the Tyne

While some of us you might call late beginners
  Have not yet even crossed the starting line !

So many legs, and all of them in front.
  It feels as though you're running on the spot ;
And so we make our grunting *exeunt*
  In what feels like a syncopated trot,
A jerky, silent epic movie-showing
  Of crowd scenes shot by Sergei Eisenstein,
A sweaty human river slowly flowing
  From Spittal Tongues towards the River Tyne
And on until at last we reach the ocean,
  A human tidal wave of wincing faces,
A festival of running in slow motion.
  Where *Nessun Dorma* meets *The Blaydon Races.*
'Howay the Lads !' the footbridge banners urge,
  Two men in tights ask, 'what aboot the lasses ?'
A sudden line of cones, the roads diverge
  And we descend beneath the underpasses,
Steep-sided like canals at emptied locks,
  To test the empty subway demagogy
As concrete roofs give back the runners' *vox*
  With cries of 'Oggy, oggy, oggy, oggy !'
And then at last the One Mile signs appear,
  A half-unwelcome sight, because although
The thought of one less mile brings half a cheer,
  It also means there's twelve miles more to go.

# 1-2
**MILES**

*" There must be a job gannin' in Sooth Sheels !"*
*(voice of spectator)*

The crowd is still too dense to pick up pace,
  You have to watch your step at every step,
And though your breathing's good you can't quite place
  The feeling in your knee as on you *schlep*
Towards the City Centre, past the Quayside,
  And up towards the bridge, the gateway South,
A fleshy flood-tide running to the seaside
  To meet the river foaming at the mouth,
Via Jarrow, Hebburn, Harton, up to Westoe,
  And all the pitless, pitiless estates
Where living is a well-thumbed manifesto
  In praise of unredeemed one party states.
Now Britain has its first North-East PM,
  But power's no longer weighed in tons of coal
Or block votes from the Durham NUM
  And 6.8% are on the dole.
Where public loss flows into private gain
  The River Tyne conjoins the Acheron,

And private profit meets with public pain,
  And Government-North-East is known as GO-NE!
Below, the swollen, muddy river flows ;
  Above, the pealing city's Sunday bells ;
And linking heaven and earth's a bridge that goes
  Across to Gateshead, where the angel dwells.


This is tomorrow's *Guardian* front page,
  The usual Tyne Bridge long-lens/aerial photo,
One of those half-true clichés which our age
  Believes can show what Britain is *in toto* -
As though the last two decades of defeat,
  Industrial neglect, decay, decline,
Could be redeemed by 80,000 feet
  In unison across the River Tyne.
Like Glasgow junkies, say, or Eton scholars
  Seen waving wads of starred GCSEs,
Or striped-shirt traders selling us for dollars,
  Ibiza clubbers stoned on whizz and Es ;
Like England fans who drink in foreign bars,
  Or vigilantes looking for a nonce,
Redundant miners doing up old cars,
  Or like New Labour branches in Provence,
Such images suggest we understand
  Our neighbours rather better than we do,
Until we see ourselves at second-hand
  And think the sepia images are true :

The Boro red, Toon Army/Maccem stripes,
  Brown ale, brown bread and avacado peas,
And all the browned-off, browning calotypes
  That separate the Tyne, the Wear, the Tees.


Part Mardi Gras, part May Day march, part Mela,
  This bannerless and minerless Big Meeting
Is like a weird, post-modern Miners' Gala
  (Without the beer, the speeches or the eating) ;
Our sweat's not spent to make the world's improvement,
  Our sponsors' banners aren't quite so exalted,
But right now we're not that much of a movement -
  This is the forward march of labour halted !
This carnival North-East's a mummer's play
  Where old Misrule rides round on Shank's mare,
The world's turned upside-down for just one day
  And every tortoise turns into a hare ;
A race with over 40,000 losers
  Where every loser gets to play the hero,
The biggest heroes are the wheel-chair users,
  And Newcastle is Rio de Janeiro !
There's something in this sweating, chugging throng
  Of runners caught in Northern monochrome,
A place and time that's yours, where you belong,
  That makes you feel as though you're almost home.
Well not quite *home* - there's still a long way yet,
  (11.1 miles to be exact)

A lot more miles of agony and sweat
  Until your knee is well and truly knacked.

# 2-3
## MILES

*" Good heavens, Mardonius, what kind are these that you have pitted us against ? It is not for money that they contend, but for glory of achievement !" (Herodotus)*

Mile two-to-three's a young, heroic time ;
  The distance yet to run is still compelling
As you begin to slowly, slowly, climb
  Towards the Park Lane roundabout and Felling.
Your legs are pumping well, both feet OK,
  That twinge in your left knee has disappeared,
You feel like you could keep this up all day,
  And now at last the road in front has cleared
Enough at least to try to up the pace,
  Enjoy the sense of movement while you can,
To greet the welcome breeze that's in your face,
  And think this run is going to run to plan.
You pass the garage forecourts' polished cars,
  An old man on his way back from the shops
Who stares at us as if we've come from Mars,
  The kids in black and white Newcastle tops.
Past Gateshead Stadium floodlights' silhouettes

You feel you could be running in Olympia,
Past javelin field, the shot and discus nets -
  Except their running kit was rather skimpier,
And while they ran in honour of Apollo,
  The god of medicine, back in rocky Delphi,
We honour *private* medicine - hard to swallow
  For those who don't think health's just for the wealthy.


This strange desire to run and run and run
  Belongs to some long centuries dead Greek farmer;
If you think distance-running's not much fun
  You should try running round in heavy armour!
To run 800m round a field
  Beneath all that required that you were fit -
That's 60 pounds of helmet, greaves and shield
  (Just like those three Green Howards in full kit).
In Elis, 40,000-plus spectators
  Cheered on their favourites through the olive trees,
Until those breathless, track-side commentators
  Like Pindar, Ceos or Bacchylides
Immediately upon the run's completion
  Immortalised the *victores ludorum*,
Their back-page poems and songs (*viz* Epinician)
  Enable us who never even saw 'em
To feel we've shared the brief athletic pride
  Of runners like the young Hippokleas,
Or three-times lucky Xenophon, who died

Four hundred years BC. Though runners pass,
The race we run is never really done,
  As in a relay race where each can hear
Beneath their racing heart-beat as they run
  The sound of long dead footsteps drawing near.


How deep this running runs in mortal hearts!
  The human race is one long-running story ;
The point we know ourselves as human starts
  When running's not for food, but fame and glory.
As verse defies extinction's cold, dark claims
  In books where long-dead lives may still be read,
So running first began as *funeral* games,
  At which the quick would entertain the dead.
Both poetry and running's done in metres,
  Both measure out their rhythmed pulse in feet ;
You do not have to be as fast as cheetahs
  Or published with the public-school elite,
You don't have to be clever, wise or witty,
  Good looks are no more help than lots of dosh,
You won't run better just because you're pretty
  Or be a better writer if you're posh.
As verse and running both are death-denying,
  They're also both a democratic art
Which anyone can try this side of dying ;
  You only need be human to take part.
Mortality is just a lame excuse

(Just like that painful throb in your left knee)
To please Poseidon or suck up to Zeus.
On which heroic note you reach mile three.

# 3-4
## MILES

*" I do not run aimlessly... I pommel my body and
subdue it." (Corinthians)*

Why do we do it ? No-one really knows,
  And least of all a runner on the run.
That said, it's safe to say we can suppose
  It isn't (*pace* Coleman) done for fun !
No-one would put themselves through this for pleasure,
  Or having done so once, come back for more,
But having fun is not the only measure
  Of what is good or what this life is for.
While others slump in garden-centre queues,
  Or snore in front of satellite TV,
Or trust in horoscopes/financial news,
  Or wait for bonus balls to set them free,
We think that life's a poor spectator-sport -
  It's best enjoyed, like running, love or art
By joining in, not watching - by the sort
  Who do not wait for this one life to start.
Just think of all the shopping trips, the cooking,
  The piles of ironing which you should have done -

Instead of which, when no-one else was looking,
  You slipped out down the alley for a run.
In rain and hail and snow and fog and sleet,
  Before the sun begins its morning climb,
In echoed footsteps running down the street
  You hear the sound of runners stealing time.


If you can run, then you can run away,
  Break out, escape, run off the beaten track,
As though each run's part training for the day
  You run towards the hills and don't come back.
That's why, perhaps, some run in fancy dress,
  As Spidermen or Roman gladiators,
As though we cannot be ourselves unless
  Disguised as mermaids, nurses, nuns and waiters.
We've fairies, pirates, teddy-boys and vicars,
  A hairy-legged and bearded ballerina,
Two women wearing only bras and knickers,
  Fred Flinstone, Barney Rubble, Princess Xena ;
We've chickens, camels, emus, eagles, llamas,
  A band of woolly vikings, one gorilla,
Some sleepy-looking runners in pyjamas,
  A woman trying to pass off as Godzilla ;
There's two blokes here dressed-up as caped-crusaders,
  Six men in kilts and four with plastic breasts,
A pair of Homer Simpsons, three Darth Vaders,
  Bikini-ed *Baywatch* girls with hairy chests.

Although they raise a laugh, and lots of money
  For hospitals which need all our support
The joke falls flat if you don't think it funny
  To pay for things our taxes should have bought.


Why do we do it ? Just to keep in trim ?
  Perhaps there's even some who like the pain !
A vain attempt at staying fit and slim ?
  (Though some would say we run because we're vain).
To prove a point maybe, or just lose weight,
  To win a bet, feel younger than you look,
Support a worthy cause, or just a mate,
  Redeem a boast your friends won't let you duck ;
To try to feel as fit as once you were
  Before your knee joints finally collapse,
To be no slower than you were last year,
  Or just impress someone (yourself perhaps).
At your age, more than two hours means disaster,
  (Unthinkable when you were in your prime) ;
With every passing year time passes faster,
  But every year you run a slower time !
How many thousand miles you must have run,
  How many thin white lines you must have seen,
And yet of all the miles you've ever done
  They were not half so long as these thirteen,
As climbing up to Heworth Metro station,
  You feel your age like rings inside a tree,

And on towards your final destination
   Beyond the rise, the long-walled cemetery.

## 4-5
### MILES

*" Fame runs before him, as the Morning Star*
*And shouts of joy salute him from afar."*
*(Dryden)*

Just less than 30 minutes on the clock
  And you're already running out of puff.
You've also hit a kind of mental block :
  In case the running wasn't tough enough,
Half-marathon arithmetic's dead hard !
  You check your watch and try to do the sums-
How many miles a minute, hours a yard-
  It's tough with just your fingers and your thumbs.
Subtract the time you took to pass the start,
  Divide by four, then times 13.1
And take off sixty ! Easy if you're smart
  But not if - just a minute though, hang on -
You try the maths again just to be sure,
  That can't be right, there must be some mistake,
Eight minute miles - that's 1hr 44 !
  The next nine miles should be a piece of cake !
Alas, from this point on your griefs begin.

The next three miles you're running on your tod,
From Pelaw on the crowds begin to thin ;
  Which leaves you feeling lonely as you plod
Towards the coast without the roadside cheers
  Of camera-waving family, friends and neighbours,
Without their urging ringing in your ears
  You're left to face your solitary labours.


To be alone and yet completely hidden
  Among so large a throng you quickly find
The most unlikely ghosts turn up unbidden
  And run beside you till they fall behind.
Up on your left's a kind of labour heaven,
  A whole estate named after those long dead -
Keir Hardie, William Morris, Pankurst, Bevan -
  Who now would be black-listed as too Red ;
There's gardens named for Lansbury, Laski, Shaw,
  For Priestley, Davie Kirkwood, AJ Cook
And half the class of 1924
  (Though fans of Ramsay Mac are out of luck),
The Webbs, George Loveless, Henderson, Will Thorne,
  MacMillan, Maggie Bondfield, Stafford Cripps,
Bright, star-lit heralds of the coming dawn
  Now clouded by our mid-day sun's eclipse.
What chance in seventy years of Milburn Mews ?
  Of Darling Drive, Blair Boulevard, Third Way ?
Will Prescott Prospect smoke with Bar-B-Qs ?

Or Mandy Mansions crumble and decay ?
Does Crony Court, Straw Street or Campbell Crescent
  Sound like the kind of place you'd like to dwell ?
Will PFI-built homes be obsolescent,
  Which first-time Byers find they cannot sell ?


We mark our passage through this world with names
  Like moon-lit pebbles on the forest track ;
Like children lost within a wood, such games
  Enable us to know the journey back.
But when the crusts of comfort all are eaten
  We have to cut a path between the trees,
And promises of sugar cannot sweeten
  The story of the forest's refugees.
You'd think by now we'd recognise the plot :
  The hungry man who leaves his kids for dead,
The little boy who's fattened for the pot,
  The bare-foot girl who bakes the witch's bread.
Though long-imagined paths are worn and old
  It doesn't mean they can't be any good ;
As long as tales of justice go untold
  The children will stay lost inside the wood.
And as this heartless world's opinion hardens
  Grand Narratives like those which once inspired
The builders who laid William Morris Gardens
  Need telling once again, for even tired
And weary runners know you can't survive

If you rely alone on flesh and bone,
Or if, as you are carried past mile five,
You think that you are running on your own.

**5-6**

**MILES**

*" Faith, I ran when I saw others run."*
*(Henry IV 1)*

From Black Bull junction down towards the Leas
  We start the long decline to Marsden Bay,
Each mile's an uphill struggle for our knees
  And yet from here it's downhill all the way!
If you've tried teaching snails the art of raffia,
  Or ever kissed a dead oran-utang,
If you've played roulette with the Russian Mafia,
  Or practised hanging loose in Pyongyang,
If you have tried to lend Bill Gates a tenner,
  Or played at hide and seek with friends on Mir,
If you have looked for Nazis in Vienna,
  Or scuba-dived for pearls off Wigan Pier,
If you have ever danced with a Venusian,
  Or microwaved a live tyrannosaur,
If you have tried to start a revolution,
  Or got off with the thing from Alien 1V,
If you have ever begged on King's Cross Station,
  Or tried to swim across the river Styx,

If you've read Kipling's 'If' to a crustacean,
  Then you've been here between miles 5 and 6,
Where hard gets tough and tough keeps getting tougher,
  Where difficult becomes just-can't-be-done,
And you'll know what it's like to really suffer
  And which is more - you'll be half-dead old son.

By now your thirst has got you at full throttle
  So you can reach the drinks before they're drunk;
There's quarter of a million water bottles
  (That's forty thousand litres to be sunk !)
And though the rule's one bottle each, you squirt
  The first one down your throat, the second goes
To cool your face, the third straight down your shirt -
  Which leaves you with sore legs and squelchy toes.
If you think running's stressful, just remember
  All those who *really* run the Great North Run,
Who've worked behind the scenes since last September
  (Whose planning for the next has just begun !)
There's nurses, doctors, hundreds of first-aiders
  And near 2,000 helpers on the day,
300 St John's Ambulance Brigaders,
  A hospital that's lent by the TA,
There's scouts and guides, police cadets and harriers,
  There's twenty mobile paramedic crews,
There's miles of traffic cones and metal barriers,
  And several hundred much-used portaloos.

This year there's 50,000 runners entered,
  They've flown here from each corner of the globe,
The paper-work would send most folk demented -
  It's either that or just the job for Job.


By now your body's really super-heating,
  The day is turning out to be a scorcher,
And last night's Chinese take-away's repeating
  (A fried-rice special kind of Chinese torture).
The terraced hills of Gateshead now behind you,
  At Whitemare Pool you leave the Felling Road,
You're in South Tyneside now, the signs remind you,
  Or 'Catherine Cookson Country' in the code
Of heritage and tourist fiction North,
  Where poverty and hunger are traditions,
A version of the past which gazes forth
  From millions of fat large print editions,
When class was class, and poor was bloody poor,
  When South was South, and rich was bloody rich,
And that's the way it will be ever more
  And lies are lies and kitsch is always kitsch.
And yet with every tatty tea-towel trail
  Depicting life as Geordie-Dvorjak grim,
Between the stitches there's another tale
  In which the North's the axle, not the rim.
And though the past's pulled down and sold for scrap,
  As every library-reader knows who borrows

The memories of bonnet, shawl and cap,
   That past makes better sense than most tomorrows.

**6-7**

**MILES**

*" For lovers ever run before the clock."*
*(The Merchant of Venice)*

Beyond the motorway, past lines of pylon,
  Through flat and scrubby urban-farmland fields,
Along Leam Lane you put another mile on -
  Which means you're almost half-way to South Shields.
From this point on each mile's another minus ;
  Each silent step the distances rewind
A song of wheezing windpipe, lung and sinus,
  The tinny beat of headphones just behind.
What kind of music gives these runners wings ?
  What sound-track does this running film require?
Rap-metal, house, free jazz or calming strings ?
  That bloody tune from *Chariots of Fire* ?
Perhaps they play a compilation tape
  Of running classics like *Young Hearts, Run Free,*
*Da Doo Run Run* or Blur's *The Great Escape,*
  And anything that's by Run DMC ?
Slow-motion *Turandot* ? Or Tears for Fears ?
  Do Dexys Midnight Runners help you run ?

Would *Born to Run* be music in your ears ?
  And do fun-runners run to Run4Fun ?
Does *Running Man* give running men a push ?
  Or playing *Keep on Running* drive you crazy ?
Could you run up that hill to Ms Kate Bush ?
  Or would you stop to *You Can't Run* (Count Basie)?


The lexicon of running is familiar
  To lovers everywhere in verse and song
(Though every mile your thinking just gets sillier,
  Such fugues as this can help you jog along),
That feeling when your pulse begin to race,
  From which your poor heart never quite recovers,
The moment when you try to give Love chase
  Is understood by runners and by lovers.
You can't beat Love, so just don't even try it
  When you catch up you find that Love has fled,
It runs you ragged, runs amok, runs riot
  And makes your heart runs rings around your head.
If you try keeping up with Atalanta,
  You know you'll never reach the finish first ;
Desire is not a jog round at a canter,
  And love is not a 100-metre burst.
It's more a patient slog, run over distance,
  If you're to stay the course, then you require
Endurance, sweat, devotion and persistence,
  Until at last you gain what you desire ;

But having won, your panting heart is changed,
  The hunter hunted now, become the prey,
Pursued by love's own hounds, confused, estranged,
  And run to ground like Actaeon at bay.


While some may run for office, power or fame,
  And some may even get to run the show,
There's many more of us whose only claim
  Is that we vindicate La Rochefoucauld :
Run out of steam, run down, run off your feet,
  Run out of luck, to seed, a running joke,
The also-rans, the ones who can't compete,
  Run of the mill, who never go for broke.
Who isn't running after something better ?
  Or isn't on the run from something worse ?
There's something in the human carburettor
  That means we can't tell forward from reverse.
Ambition, struggle, labour, love and friends -
  The stuff that makes a human life complete -
The thought that they're just round the next few bends
  Puts extra mileage in your flagging feet.
How real they seem, the things that we pursue,
  As real as those from which we run away,
And yet somehow they all converge in you
  As disappointment, failure and dismay.
We start like Billy Whizz or Don Quixote,
  And then like Aesop's hare we fall asleep,

And wake too late, as always, like Coyote
  In time to see our dreams run past - Beep Beep !

# 7-8

**MILES**

*" Thou run's a hapless race*
*To win despair. No crown*
*Awaits success, but leaden gods look down*
*On thee, with evil face.."*
*(Robert Louis Stephenson)*

There's not much pain between miles seven and eight,
  You're running now on automatic pilot,
You try to tell yourself you're looking great
  (Part cardiac-red, part hypothermic violet) ;
Although both knees are really stiff and sore,
  And there is something wrong with both your hips,
Although your right big-toe is rubbing raw,
  Your mouth's so parched, you cannot lick your lips,
Although your legs are watery and weak,
  Your running shorts are rubbing in your crutch,
Although your thermostat is up the creek,
  Compared to what's to come, it's nothing much.
Outside the Robin Hood the Sunday-drinkers
  Lift pints as though they know how it disheartens.
We stare ahead as though we're wearing blinkers

And scowl as if to say we're tough as Spartans.
Heads down, we run like cattle to the slaughter,
  Your powers of self-denial fit to burst,
Just past mile eight there's showers and bottled water
  Where you can try to slake your desert thirst.
The thought of water helps to keep you going,
  You grit your teeth and stare down at the kerb,
There's something in your bowels that's now yo-yoing
  (This probably requires another verb).

In Y2K the Great North Run is twenty,
  And so we run in double celebration,
A Happy Birthday conga *(lentamente)*
  Howay the lads ! O happy combination !
Like Disney's lemmings sprinting for the cliff
  Or headless chickens heading for a fall
We run this *fin de siecle* run as if
  We've got that MM virus after all.
We run to greet the next one thousand years
  Before we think too much about the last,
Which ended as this one's begun, in tears,
  For now the future's certain as the past.
The record is a miserable procession,
  Unedifying as our claims are noble :
Intolerance, injustice and oppression,
  The usual stuff (except they've now gone global).
We run to mark the dawning of an era

Of poverty and hunger, debt and war,
In which the hope of ages is no nearer,
 The rich still have a head-start on the poor
And History is like a dismal relay
 In which the wealthy batten on the weak,
For *fugit tempus inreparabile*
 And in the long run things are looking bleak.


Your sense of time is starting to unravel,
 The road in front of you begins to melt,
So many minutes still through which to travel,
 (You know how Zeno's arrow must have felt !)
How strong our sense of living left to right,
 Of moving in a line from first to last,
The feeling that we travel as we write
 And run towards the future from the past.
Suppose it was the opposite direction
 And memory allowed us to rehearse
Tomorrow's blushing follies to perfection
 Would yesterday's mistakes seem any worse ?
Imagine running back towards the past,
 Where every step led back to your beginnings,
As though the rewind button were stuck fast
 And death was just the start of every innings.
A Martin Amis-scripted *Ground Hog Day*,
 Where knackered runners run from hard to easy,
Until we tumble backwards all the way

To cross the start, dead fit instead of wheezy,
To celebrate with platefuls of spaghetti
    And then a sober, quiet and early night,
A Great North Run where runners get less sweaty,
    From Zdleish Thous to Ulssacwen nuppo nite!

# 8-9

## MILES

*" Here, you see, it takes all the running you can do, to keep in the same place. If you want to get somewhere else, you must run at least twice as fast as that !"*
*(Alice Through the Looking Glass)*

By now you're having second second-thoughts
  Your feet are sore, there's pain in both your knees
It's surely time to take up gentler sports,
  The sort that do not make you groan and wheeze.
If only that weren't such an understatement !
  Your breathing is the least of your concerns ;
This torment has no prospect of abatement,
  You've past the painful point of no return.
Somewhere round here is where the spirit dies ;
  The agonizing, all consuming pain
Is not just in your calves and back and thighs,
  But buried in the centre of your brain.
How can you put in words the mind's ordeal ?
  Distress, discomfort, misery and grief,
Accumulating slowly till you feel
  A tortured senseless ache beyond belief.

If legs and feet may be described as bored
  (As after eight long miles you think they may)
Then so your brain hurts when it's been ignored
  So long its emptied faculties decay,
Deprived of sense, you half-hallucinate,
  And surf and scroll your files from A-Z ;
In other words, between miles nine and eight
  You find you're slowly going off your head.

You force yourself to read the backs of vests,
  The sponsors' logos, acronyms and names,
You send your memory off on hopeless quests
  And idiotic arithmetic games :
You try to estimate how many paces
  You'll take to reach that bus-stop by the lights,
How many training shoes have coloured laces,
  How many runners run in running tights ;
You count the lamp-posts, legs, and try to guess
  Which feet belong to women, which to men,
The ratio of shorts to fancy dress,
  The register at school when you were ten.
And so your mind begins its backwards trek
  Re-winding long-lost knowledge shot in cine :
How many bushels used to make a peck,
  How many pennies used to make a guinea,
The names of Saturn's moons, the US states,
  How many football league grounds you've attended,

Prime Ministers and Monarchs (with their dates)
  The names of all the people you've offended ;
How many gills per pint, or pints per quart,
  How many yards are in a mile or a chain,
The way to calculate the root of nought,
  How many miles before you are insane.


Approaching Simonside there's bottled water :
  West Harton mirage ! Brockley Whins oasis !
We drink more water than we really ought to
  And pour it on our upturned beetroot faces.
You stagger on, half-drunk on $H_2O$,
  Through tepid showers that feel like mountain streams,
Round dizzy roundabouts that spin as though
  The world is not as stable as it seems :
And England win the ashes in Australia,
  The IMF writes off all Third World Debts,
And Tony Blair admits the Dome a failure,
  And Pinochet confesses to regrets ;
The Boro get to win the League at last,
  The ozone layer's magically restored,
And Englands' World Cup hopefuls aren't out-classed
  And scientists say the ice-caps have unthawed ;
The Tories lose their last Westminster seat,
  And Rupert Murdoch's papers go unsold,
A billion hungry humans get to eat,
  And poor old Mrs Thatcher is paroled.

O happy day ! Imagined cornucopia !
  Where every runner runs as in their youth,
Where every step you take's towards utopia
  And every tired utopian runs in truth.

**MILES**

*" Our wills and fate do so contrary run."*
*(Hamlet)*

Down John Reid Road and up past Brockley Whins
  There's always one more roundabout ahead,
Here's where the cheering roadside crowd begins
  To change its stripes from black and white to red.
We run towards the tunnel's healing waters,
  More drinks - and best of all - a free urinal,
An army of supporters to support us,
  To cheer us on as though towards the final.
So many number 10s and number 9s !
  So many home defeats and so few wins !
The optimism of the will combines
  In all these would-be Shearers, Phillips, Quinns.
All these who have inherited the dream
  Of bringing back the FA Cup from Wembley
Could maybe teach the vision-lacking team
  Who call themselves the regional assembly
A thing or two about the trick of losing,
  That endless journey back down Wembley Way

Made bearable somehow just by refusing
  To think you won't be back another day.
Within the silent crowd behind the goal
  You come to know what being patient means,
Enduring as uneconomic coal
  Beneath these levelled, landscaped, pit-head greens.


The throbbing in your knees now's pretty livid,
  You doubt your hamstrung legs could feel much worse,
The pain inside your brain is now so vivid
  You fear you'll only reach home in a hearse.
Mile nine-to-ten's a time for desperate measures,
  The mile in which all runners apprehend
That when the body's stripped of all its pleasures
  You cannot help but contemplate its end :
Each step you take's one less before you're finished,
  A runner's always running out of breath,
Dismay and pain and grief are undiminished
  Until the race abruptly ends in death.
A runner's life is like that winter sparrow
  You know the one, the *passer* used by Bede
(And everyone who since has been to Jarrow)
  To illustrate the passing-through-ist creed :
The bird that flies into the fire-lit room,
  Attracted by the warmth within the hall,
And out again into that waiting gloom
  Of which we can't say anything at all.

But we're not passing through, we're here to stay,
  This running's not the same as passing by,
Each step you take's imprinted on the clay
  Which holds us here until the day we die.


Did thoughts like these beset Phidippides,
  The very first long distance-running martyr ?
Did he endure such problems with his knees
  When he ran straight from Athens down to Sparta?
Did Schwarzenegger (*Running Man*) feel knackered?
  Mel Gibson (in *Gallipoli*) perspire ?
And was Tom Hanks in *Forest Gump* cream-crackered ?
  Did Ben Cross sweat in *Chariots of Fire*?
Does Paula Radcliffe wish that she were faster ?
  And has John Mutai ever felt a flop ?
Is Joao Lopes ever sick of pasta ?
  And does Tegla Loroupe wish she could stop ?
The fears on which all distance-runners thrive
  Are those which help inspire all living things :
Each painful yard reminds you you're alive,
  And that although you're mortal you have wings,
The kind of knowledge that still actuates
  The wheel chair sprinters, spinning off ahead,
The chair-bound runners pushed along by mates,
  Unsighted runners, running on a thread,
And all of us composed of flesh and bone
  Who almost from the moment we can crawl

Suspect the fear of death's for us alone
  And that we're only human after all.

# 10 - 11
## MILES

*" The generations of living things pass in a short time and like runners hand on the torch of life."*
*(Lucretius)*

A thousand watches bleep on every side
  Announcing news that's either bad or grim,
A thousand runners re-adjust their stride
  As prospects for a record time grow dim.
Ten miles in 1 hr 30's still *OK*
  Except it means you must be quickly slowing ;
All hopes of Personal Bests are put away,
  The only thing that counts is keeping going.
The qualities on which you now must draw
  To get you through the next 5,000 metres
Are less to do with stamina and more
  *The Pilgrim's Progress* or the *Bhagavad-Gitas* -
A patient, plodding, Northern kind of Zen,
  The toughest track according to Alf Tupper
(That Existential tough whose regimen
  Was based on bags of fish and chips for supper !)
A speechless contemplation of the beat,

The clashing rhythms of the body's fevers,
The pumping blood, the thump of legs and feet,
  Of over 40,000 heavy breathers ;
An obstinate and silent perseverance,
  A thoughtless state that's almost transcendental
(Though judging from your desperate appearance
  Some might suspect that you are simply mental).


And so to Harton Nook, the row of shops,
  A gang of girls around a ghetto-blaster,
Some cheerful kids who wave from bus-stop tops
  Whose cheering briefly gets you running faster.
Gorse Avenue is on your right-hand side,
  Where Harry Heslop's ghost may still be found,
The house in which he wrote the books which tried
  To show the world the world beneath the ground.
Forgotten now, his novels once were praised
  In London, Moscow, Rome and Montreal,
By well-read critics who were just amazed
  To read a miner who could write at all.
A 'major miner writer' ! How alarming !
  The homonym suggests the somewhat squeamish
Response of those who found his prose-style charming,
  But wouldn't want to spend a day at Beamish.
A major writer and a Durham miner,
  He took the speech of pulpit, union, choir,
And knicked and kirved it into something finer,

A tongue with which to set the world on fire,
To lick the darkness of the uncut seams
  Of revolution, justice, labour's right,
And put in words the untold coal-face dreams
  That crawl beneath the surface in the night.


There's something in this North-East running tribe
  Of which old Reds like Harry would approve,
A set of sweaty virtues which describe
  A kind of Northern Rising on the move ;
The sport of kings, of course, it's clearly not,
  (Do monarchs ever sweat, or get dishevelled ?)
We are the *hoi-poloi*, the *sans-culottes*,
  For whom all class distinction's swiftly levelled.
This is the lost Republic of sore knees
  A comradeship of moaners and complainers,
The union of the Tyne, the Wear and Tees
  Where runners run as equals in their trainers.
There's no sign in our ranks of Millbank spinners,
  Or sycophants with public school-boy vowels,
Of NATO spokesmen or roll-over winners,
  Fox-hunting toffs, or fans of Enoch Powell's ;
No canonised dead princesses and Tsars,
  Poujadist tabloid readers who can't read,
Asylum seeker-seekers smashing bars
  (And anyone who has the prefix *paed*).
In short, this run contains a kind of pattern,

Co-operative, inclusive and self-taught,
A vision where all hierarchies flatten,
  And rank and class and deference count for nought.

# 11 - 12
## MILES

*" They shall run and not be weary."*
*(Isaiah)*

The road climbs Marsden Hill towards the pub
　Where mid-day drinkers guzzle in the sun
And gorge themselves on plates of Sunday grub,
　While you're supposed to get on with the run !
Like thirsty Tantalus the nearness heightens
　Your sense that you'd could drink the North Sea dry,
This kind of torture Zeus reserved for Titans
　Or those so bad they weren't allowed to die,
Like Ixion upon the turning rack,
　Or liverish Prometheus on the rocks,
Like Atlas with the world upon his back,
　Or Sisyphus in vest and running socks.
And yet those tortured creatures were survivors,
　They did not have the option of defeat ;
There's something in the taste of old salivas,
　That keeps you running even when you're beat ;
Between desire, exhaustion and despair

Is something more than fresh testosterone ;
The world's not made from what we've left to spare
  When we have met the needs of flesh and bone,
We make ourselves with every step we take
  And what we make ourselves this world becomes ;
And art is more than icing on the cake,
  Although arts-funding usually gets the crumbs !


Here art for all is more than distant rumours,
  It's isn't just a slogan used by funders ;
Like running, it's for doers not consumers,
  Who given half a chance come up with wonders.
Along Prince Edward Road there's cooling waters,
  There's kids with hands held out for you to slap,
Old ladies well supplied with orange quarters,
  And folk to hose you down, or just to clap.
And thanks to Northern Arts and super-Nova
  We run this year to string quartets and jazz,
A carnival to dance to when it's over,
  Millennial (but Dome-less) razzmatazz ;
This year the route is lined with flags and banners
  To warm us on a cold October day,
There's 20,000 folk to sing Hosannas,
  And bands to entertain us on the way,
There's drummers, indie-combos, bag-pipes, blues,
  And poetry from schools that line the route
There's tableaux, bill-boards, papier-mache shoes,

   Balloons, cartoons and tunes that constitute
A festival of sound and colour made
   By hundreds of beginners, pros and amateurs,
With art of every shape and every shade
   (Including these iambic-ish pentameters !)

Of all the arts the need to write run's deepest,
   An impulse that all runners understand,
(In funding terms it's certainly the cheapest)
   To leave some mark, some footprints in the sand.
You might expect that in this age of masses -
   Mass culture, media, literacy and sports -
There'd be more athletes from the writing classes,
   More poets dressed in vest and running shorts.
If writing verse resembled losing calories,
   Slim volumes wouldn't seem so limp and tired,
And poets who enjoy the plumpest salaries
   Would not be those who seem the least inspired.
It's said that Philip Larkin kept in trim
   By exercising on his mountain bike,
While TS Eliot worked out in the gym,
   And Wordsworth liked to run up Scafell Pike ;
John Betjeman was into steeple-chasing ;
   And Ted Hughes used to do the Iron Man,
The Martian poets are good at three-legged racing,
   Howay the lads ! Just watch those poets gan !
Though some might think the parallel is tenuous,

The best art's made, like any sport, from sweat,
Like running, it's as pointless as it's strenuous,
    (And this must be as pointless as you get !)

# 12-13
## MILES

" *So much I feel my genial spirits droop,*
*My hopes all flat, nature within me seems*
*In all her functions weary of herself ;*
*My race of glory runs, and race of shame,*
*And I shall shortly be with them that rest.*"
(*Milton*)

And so at last you pass the twelve mile sign,
  Your body somehow switched to automatic,
A spaced-out, weightless, brain-dead, aerodyne
  Somewhere between immovable and static.
Both knee-caps now are in a metal vice
  And both your ankles feel extremely tender
Your aching neck is in a grip of ice,
  Your tortured body's screaming for surrender.
By now the only thing you really know
  Is that you've lost all sense of time and place ;
Though there's just 1.1 miles still to go,
  For all you know you're now in outer space.
You could be on the dark side of the Moon ;

Or maybe you have died, and this is hell ?
Inside your pain-lined solipsist's cocoon
   It isn't really possible to tell.
If this is Earth, these must be *Homo Saps*
   (Except the wisdom part does not ring true !)
Your rational mind is verging on collapse -
   If this is Earth, then what on earth are you ?
Compared to you these others seem so young,
   Such graceful creatures, effortlessly flying,
While judging from the feeling in your lungs
   This is what humans feel when they are dying.


The huge North Sea's now massing on your right
   Its freezing spray an anaesthetic blast
That helps you face the miserable sight
   Of runners who have finished, running past
In this year's vest towards the Metro station .
   You envy them their triumph, and delude
Your weary self with dreams of relaxation,
   Of being home - hot baths, hot drink, hot food -
Although for slow-coach finishers the prize
   Is Sunday afternoon in car-park queues
As every hypothermic runner tries
   To make it home before the evening news.
You pass the banners urging 'Come on Mam',
   'Away Our Terry', 'Happy Birthday Dad'.
'You're Nearly There', 'Well Done to Kev and Sam',

'Toon Army Stan' and 'Auntie Jan You're Mad'.
You somehow blunder on, you can't say how,
  Sustained by desperation and despair,
A helpful voice shouts, 'Not much further now'
  Although to be quite honest you don't care ;
Your only thought by now's the certain fact
  That when you're through this suffering and pain,
Your resolution will be still intact :
  To never, ever, run this run again.

Three hundred yards to go and then you're done,
  You grit your teeth and keep on keeping on,
Of all the many miles you've ever run
  There's none as painful as the next . *1*
At last the gantry-clock appears in view,
  But there's as many runners on the road
As at the start, and all in front of you !
  (They've either speeded up or else you've slowed).
You try to sprint, but dead legs won't obey,
  The pace increases, then slows down again ;
The electronic seconds blip away,
  12 seconds left to beat your time - then 10,
Then 9, then 8, then you're below the clock,
  Abrupt and sudden end of all your hopes ;
You try to brake, exhausted and in shock,
  And stumble on towards the funnelled ropes,
Where someone takes your number, with 'Well done,'

An understatement which you disregard,
For now the grief and misery is run,
  In retrospect it wasn't all that hard !
You don't know why some people make a fuss,
  As, stumbling on as though you're not quite sober
Towards the T-shirts and the baggage bus,
  You promise that you'll be back next October...